100th Day of School

By EMMA CARLSON BERNE

Illustrations by CHARLIE ALDER

Music by MARK MALLMAN

CANTATA
LEARNING

WWW.CANTATALEARNING.COM

CANTATA LEARNING

Published by Cantata Learning
1710 Roe Crest Drive
North Mankato, MN 56003
www.cantatalearning.com

Library of Congress Cataloging-in-Publication Data
Names: Berne, Emma Carlson, author. | Alder, Charlie, illustrator. | Mallman,
  Mark, composer.
Title: 100th day of school / by Emma Carlson Berne ; illustrated by
  Charlie Alder ; music by Mark Mallman.
Other titles: One hundredth day of school
Description: North Mankato, MN : Cantata Learning, [2018] | Series: Holidays
  in rhythm and rhyme | Audience: Ages 5–7. | Audience: K to grade 3.
Identifiers: LCCN 2017017526 (print) | LCCN 2017035542 (ebook) | ISBN
  9781684101641 (ebook) | ISBN 9781684101368 (hardcover : alk. paper) | ISBN
  9781684101894 (pbk. : alk. paper)
Subjects: LCSH: Hundredth Day of School--Juvenile literature. |
  Schools--Juvenile literature. | Holidays--Juvenile literature.
Classification: LCC LB3533 (ebook) | LCC LB3533 .B47 2018 (print) | DDC
  394.261--dc23
LC record available at https://lccn.loc.gov/2017017526

Book design and art direction, Tim Palin Creative
Editorial direction, Kellie M. Hultgren
Music direction, Elizabeth Draper
Music arranged and produced by Mark Mallman

Printed in the United States of America in North Mankato, Minnesota.
122017   0378CGS18

ACCESS THE MUSIC!
SCAN CODE WITH MOBILE APP
CANTATALEARNING.COM

TIPS TO SUPPORT LITERACY AT HOME

WHY READING AND SINGING WITH YOUR CHILD IS SO IMPORTANT

Daily reading with your child leads to increased academic achievement. Music and songs, specifically rhyming songs, are a fun and easy way to build early literacy and language development. Music skills correlate significantly with both phonological awareness and reading development. Singing helps build vocabulary and speech development. And reading and appreciating music together is a wonderful way to strengthen your relationship.

READ AND SING EVERY DAY!

TIPS FOR USING CANTATA LEARNING BOOKS AND SONGS DURING YOUR DAILY STORY TIME

1. As you sing and read, point out the different words on the page that rhyme. Suggest other words that rhyme.

2. Memorize simple rhymes such as Itsy Bitsy Spider and sing them together. This encourages comprehension skills and early literacy skills.

3. Use the questions in the back of each book to guide your singing and storytelling.

4. Read the included sheet music with your child while you listen to the song. How do the music notes correlate to the words of the song?

5. Sing along on the go and at home. Access music by scanning the QR code on each Cantata book. You can also stream or download the music for free to your computer, smartphone, or mobile device.

Devoting time to daily reading shows that you are available for your child. Together, you are building language, literacy, and listening skills.

Have fun reading and singing!

One hundred days is a lot of learning! That is why students and their teachers **celebrate** the one hundredth school day. This day is usually in January or February. Students bring in one hundred small objects. They might eat one hundred tiny snacks. On the one hundredth day of school, students might do a math lesson about counting to one hundred. They might read a book about a little girl who has one hundred dresses.

Turn the page and sing along to celebrate one hundred days of learning!

The hundredth day of school has come.

It's wintertime outside.

Let's think of all the things we've learned
and celebrate with pride!

We studied hard and learned together for one hundred days.

We listened to our teachers,
and now it's time to play!

Our teacher gave us **homework**:
bring in one hundred things.

We found **acorns**, beads, and coins,
even bits of string.

We studied hard and learned together
for one hundred days.

We listened to our teachers,
and now it's time to play!

12

We have raisins for our snack today.

Into the bowl we reach.

We scoop them out in bunches
and count one hundred each.

We studied hard and learned together
for one hundred days.

We listened to our teachers,
and now it's time to play!

The party isn't over yet.

Our teacher says, "Math time!"

We count up to one hundred
with pennies, nickels, and dimes.

We studied hard and learned together
for one hundred days.

We listened to our teachers,
and now it's time to play!

SONG LYRICS
100th Day of School

The hundredth day of school has come.
It's wintertime outside.
Let's think of all the things we've learned
and celebrate with pride!

We studied hard and learned together
for one hundred days.
We listened to our teachers,
and now it's time to play!

Our teacher gave us homework:
bring in one hundred things.
We found acorns, beads, and coins,
even bits of string.

We studied hard and learned together
for one hundred days.
We listened to our teachers,
and now it's time to play!

We have raisins for our snack today.
Into the bowl we reach.
We scoop them out in bunches
and count one hundred each.

We studied hard and learned together
for one hundred days.
We listened to our teachers,
and now it's time to play!

The party isn't over yet.
Our teacher says, "Math time!"
We count up to one hundred
with pennies, nickels, and dimes.

We studied hard and learned together
for one hundred days.
We listened to our teachers,
and now it's time to play!

100th Day of School

Funk Pop
Mark Mallman

Verse

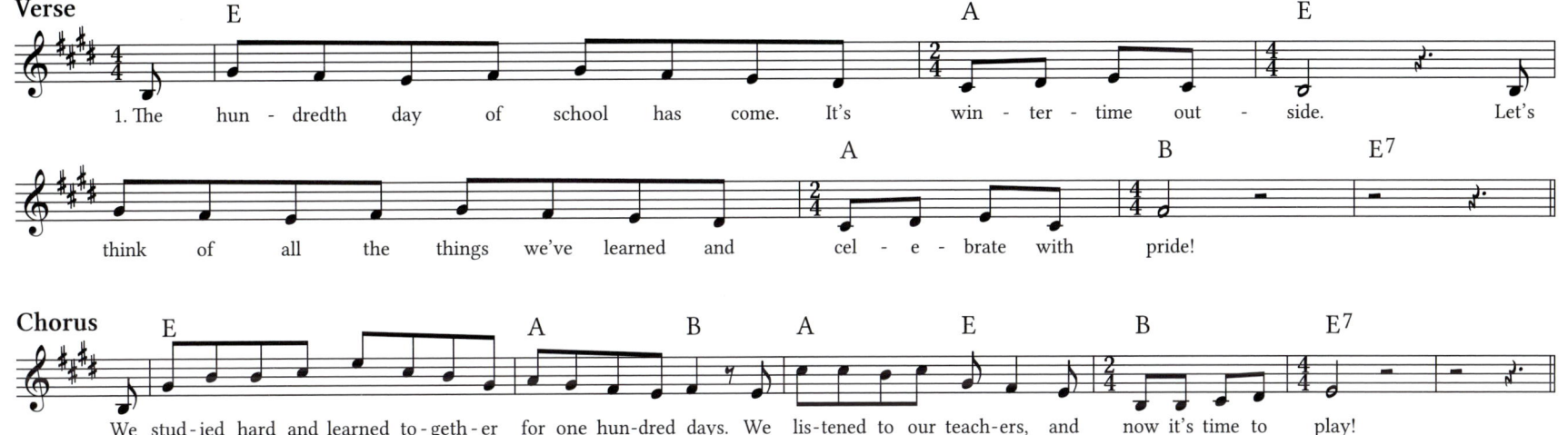

1. The hun-dredth day of school has come. It's win-ter-time out-side. Let's
think of all the things we've learned and cel-e-brate with pride!

Chorus

We stud-ied hard and learned to-geth-er for one hun-dred days. We lis-tened to our teach-ers, and now it's time to play!

Verse 2
Our teacher gave us homework:
bring in one hundred things.
We found acorns, beads, and coins,
even bits of string.

Chorus

Verse 3
We have raisins for our snack today.
Into the bowl we reach.
We scoop them out in bunches
and count one hundred each.

Chorus

Verse 4
The party isn't over yet.
Our teacher says, "Math time!"
We count up to one hundred
with pennies, nickels, and dimes.

Chorus

Outro

23

GLOSSARY

acorns—the round, hard nuts from an oak tree

celebrate—to mark a special day with a party or special events

homework—school work that a teacher gives students to do at home

GUIDED READING ACTIVITIES

1. The one hundredth day of school is about celebrating learning. What is your favorite part of learning at school? Why do you like this part?

2. This song describes several activities children do on the one hundredth day of school. Can you think of a new school activity for the one hundredth day?

3. Invent a new school holiday. Say why your holiday would be fun and useful for children to celebrate in school.

TO LEARN MORE

Arena, Jen. *100 Snowmen*. New York: Scholastic, 2013.

Estes, Eleanor. *The Hundred Dresses*. New York: Harcourt, 1944.

Wallace, Nancy Elizabeth. *Ready, Set, 100th Day!* New York: Scholastic, 2011